LIMESTONE-CENTRAL SCHOOL LIBRARY

CATS
SET II

Exotic Shorthair Cats

Stuart A. Kallen

ABDO & Daughters

visit us at
www.abdopub.com

Published by Abdo & Daughters, 4940 Viking Drive, Suite 622, Edina, Minnesota 55435. Copyright © 1998 by Abdo Consulting Group, Inc., Pentagon Tower, P.O. Box 36036, Minneapolis, Minnesota 55435 USA. International copyrights reserved in all countries. No part of this book may be reproduced in any form without written permission from the publisher.

Printed in the United States.

Photo credits: Peter Arnold, Inc., Animals Animals, TICA

Edited by Lori Kinstad Pupeza

Library of Congress Cataloging-in-Publication Data

Kallen, Stuart A., 1955-
    Exotic shorthair cats / Stuart A. Kallen.
    p. cm. -- (Cats. Set II)
    Includes index.
    Summary: Describes the physical characteristics, behavior, and life cycle of these loving, playful cats.
    ISBN 1-56239-581-5
    1. Exotic shorthair cat--Juvenile literature. [1. Exotic shorthair cat. 2. Cats.] I. Title. II. Series: Kallen, Stuart A., 1955- Cats. Set II.
SF449.E93K35   1998
636.8'26--dc20
                                                        95-48189
                                                        CIP
                                                        AC

Contents

Lions, Tigers, and Cats 4

Exotic Shorthair 6

Qualities 8

Coat and Color 10

Size 12

Care 14

Feeding 16

Kittens 18

Buying a Kitten 20

Glossary 22

Internet Sites 23

Index 24

Lions, Tigers, and Cats

Few animals are as beautiful and graceful as cats. And all cats are related. From the wild lions of Africa to common house cats, all belong to the family **Felidae**. Wild cats are found almost everywhere. They include cheetahs, jaguars, lynx, ocelots, and **domestic** cats.

Cats were first domesticated around 5,000 years ago in the Middle East. Although tamed by humans, house cats still think and act like their bigger cousins.

Tigers are related to domestic cats.

Exotic Shorthair

Exotic shorthair cats are just like Persian cats, except for their shorter coats. They were first developed in the early 1960s when breeders crossed Persian cats with American shorthairs.

Like the Persian, the exotic shorthair cat has a compact body, short legs, and a pushed-in face. Although it is a shorthair, its hair is slightly longer than the American shorthair's. In the early years, Burmese and British shorthairs were also used for breeding. This practice was stopped in 1968. The exotic shorthair has been an **official breed** in the **Cat Fanciers Association (CFA)** since 1966.

Exotic shorthairs are becoming very popular. These cats have the beautiful look of longhaired Persians. But unlike the Persian, the coat of the exotic shorthair cat is easy to **groom** and care for.

Exotic shorthairs are related to Persian cats.

Qualities

Exotic shorthairs have "laid-back" personalities. They are very calm and quiet. They rarely get too excited. This makes them good with children—even young ones. When picked up, an exotic shorthair might nudge and butt its head against the face of its owner while purring loudly. Exotics usually don't jump up to high places. This means they won't climb up curtains or window screens.

Exotic shorthairs have the sweet expressions of Persians, but they don't need the extra work of **grooming**. They are loving, playful, and make great pets.

Opposite page: Exotic shorthairs do not like to jump up to high places.

Coat and Color

The coat of the exotic shorthair is dense, plush, soft and medium in length. Exotic shorthairs may be all the colors of American shorthairs, with Persians included. This may be as many as 50 colors and markings. But they may not be lavender or chocolate if they are going to fit in with the **Cat Fanciers Association's** (**CFA**'s) rules.

Exotics may be white, black, blue, red, cream, silver, chinchilla, or shell cameo. They may be tortoiseshell. Exotics may be classic or mackerel tabby pattern in silver, red, brown, cream, or cameo. They may be patched tabby pattern in brown, silver, or blue.

Most exotic shorthairs have copper eyes. But they may have eye colors that match their fur. Their noses and paw pads should also match the coloring of their coats.

Exotic shorthairs come in many different colors.

Size

Exotic shorthairs are medium to large size cats. They weigh from 7 to 12 pounds (3 to 6 kg)—or even more. They have dense, compact bodies set low on their legs. Their tails are thick, short, and straight. Exotics have deep, wide chests, large rears, and short, thick legs. Their paws are small and round.

Exotics have large, round heads with thick necks. They have the pushed-in faces of Persians. They have well-spaced, round eyes. Their ears are small and rounded. Their snubbed noses are short and broad. Exotics have full cheeks with broad, powerful jaws.

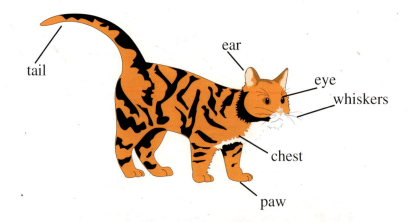

Exotic shorthairs are considered medium to large sized cats.

Care

Like any pet, an exotic shorthair needs a lot of love and attention. They make fine pets. But they still have some of their wild instincts. Cats are natural hunters and do well exploring outdoors.

A **scratching post** where the cat can sharpen its claws saves furniture from damage. A cat will bury its waste and should be trained to use a litter box. The box needs to be cleaned every day. Cats lick their coats to stay clean. Exotics have an easy-to-care-for coat that should be lightly brushed every day. They love to play. A ball, **catnip**, or a loose string will keep a kitten busy for hours.

Cats should be **spayed** or **neutered** unless you are planning to breed them. Females can have dozens of kittens a year. Males will spray very unpleasant odors indoors and out if not fixed.

Exotic shorthairs love to play.

Feeding

    Most cats that live indoors can survive fine on dried cat food. Water should always be available. Cats are meat eaters. Cats that are allowed to roam outdoors can hunt for their food. They will eat birds and rodents.

    Hard bones that do not splinter help keep a cat's teeth and mouth clean. Although they love milk, it might cause cats to become ill. Ask a **veterinarian** for the best food for your cat.

Despite popular belief, milk is not always good for cats.

Kittens

A female cat is **pregnant** for about 65 days. When kittens are born, there may be from two to eight babies. The average exotic shorthair has four kittens per litter. Kittens are blind and helpless for the first several weeks.

After about three weeks kittens will start crawling and playing. At this time they may be given cat food. After about a month, kittens will run, wrestle, and play games.

If the cat has a **pedigree**, kittens should be **registered** and given papers at this time. At 10 weeks the kittens are old enough to be sold or given away. Exotics are chunky when born. Their faces flatten out and their ears stand up after about four or five months.

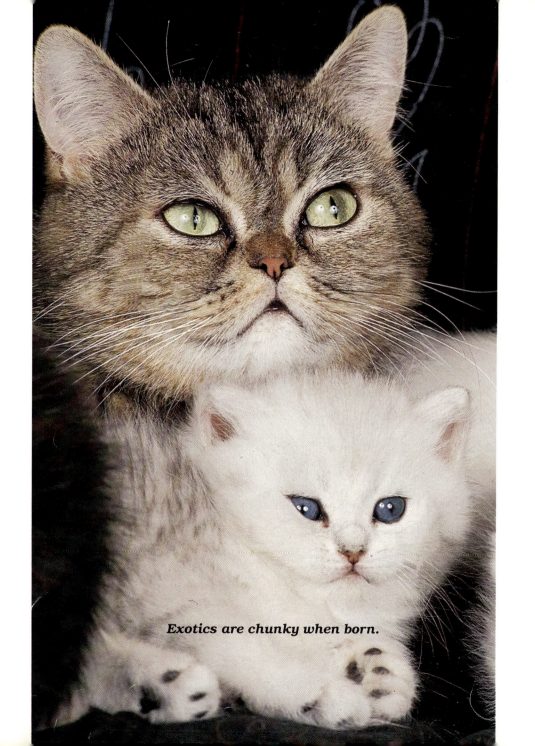
Exotics are chunky when born.

Buying a Kitten

The best place to get an exotic shorthair is from a breeder. Cat shows are also good places to find kittens. Next you must decide if you want a simple pet or a show winner. A basic exotic can cost $150. A blue-ribbon winner can cost as much as $1,500. When you buy an exotic shorthair, you should get **pedigree** papers that **register** the animal with the **Cat Fanciers Association**.

When buying a kitten, check it closely for signs of good health. The ears, nose, mouth, and fur should be clean. Its eyes should be bright and clear. The cat should be alert and interested in its surroundings. A healthy kitten will move around with its head held high.

Opposite page: A family of exotic shorthairs.

Glossary

breed/official breed - a kind of cat, an exotic shorthair is a breed of cat. An official breed is a breed that is recognized by special cat organizations.
Cat Fanciers Association (CFA) - a group that sets the standards for the breeds of cats.
catnip - the dried leaves and stems of a plant of the mint family, used as a stuffing for cats' toys because cats are stimulated by and drawn to its strong smell.
domestic/domesticated - tamed or adapted to home life.
Felidae - Latin name given to the cat family.
grooming - cleaning.
hairballs - balls of fur that gather in a cat's stomach after grooming.
neutered - a male cat that is neutered cannot get a female cat pregnant.
non-pedigree - an animal without a record of an amimal's ancestors.
pedigree - a record of an animal's ancestors.
pregnant - when a female cat has kittens growing inside it.
register - to add a cat to an official list of a breed.
scratching post - a post for a cat to scratch on, which is usually made out of wood or covered with carpet, so the cat can wear down its nails.
spayed - a female cat that is spayed cannot have kittens.
veterinarian - an animal doctor.

Internet Sites

All About Cats
http://w3.one.net/~mich/index.html
See pictures of cats around the net, take a cat quiz to win prizes, and there is even a cat advice column. This is a fun and lively site.

Cat Fanciers Website
http://www.fanciers.com/
Information on breeds, shows, genetics, breed rescue, catteries and other topics. This is a very informative site, including clubs and many links.

Cats Homepage
http://www.cisea.it/pages/gatto/meow.htm
Page for all cat lovers. Cat photo gallery, books and more. This site has music and chat rooms, it's a lot of fun.

Cats Cats Cats
http://www.geocities.com/Heartland/Hills/5157/
This is just a fun site with pictures of cats, links, stories, and other cat stuff.

These sites are subject to change. Go to your favorite search engine and type in CATS for more sites.

PASS IT ON

Tell Others Something Special About Your Pet

To educate readers around the country, pass on interesting tips about animals, maybe a fun story about your animal or pet, and little unknown facts about animals. We want to hear from you!
To get posted on ABDO & Daughters website, E-mail us at "animals@abdopub.com"

Index

A

American shorthair 6, 10
attention 14

B

birds 16
body 6, 12
bones 16
breeder 6, 20
British shorthair 6
Burmese 6

C

Cat Fanciers Association 6, 20
catnip 14
cheetahs 4
claws 14
coat 6, 10, 14
color 10

D

domestic cat 4

E

ears 12, 18, 20
eyes 10, 12, 20

F

face 6, 8, 12, 18
Felidae 4
fur 10, 20

H

humans 4
hunt 14, 16

J

jaguars 4

K

kittens 14, 18, 20

L

legs 6, 12
lions 4
litter box 14
love 14, 16
lynx 4

M

Middle East 4
milk 16

N

neutered 14

O

ocelots 4

P

paws 12
pedigree 18, 20
Persian cats 6
personality 8
pur 8

R

register 18, 20
rodents 16

S

scratching post 14

T

tail 12

W

water 16